The Waitress Handbook

by
Cathryn Rutledge

authorHOUSE™

1663 LIBERTY DRIVE, SUITE 200
BLOOMINGTON, INDIANA 47403
(800) 839-8640
WWW.AUTHORHOUSE.COM

First published by AuthorHouse 11/22/05

ISBN: 1-4208-8602-9 (sc)

Printed in the United States of America
Bloomington, Indiana

This book is printed on acid-free paper.

Contents

Chapter One
Introduction

In the restaurant business of today there is mostly mass confusion among employees because most are not properly taught. Thirty or more years ago all waitresses, cooks and dishwashers were taught the same way.

It was not uncommon in the early 1960's for children to start working as soon as they were mature enough to work. Commercial automatic dishwashers were not available in most restaurants in those days. Children as young as age eleven started in the restaurant business earning fifty cents an hour washing dishes by hand in a three compartment sink after school. This also included side work, such as chopping onions for hamburger relish and/or peeling potatoes in five gallon buckets for French fries.

In the early 1960's all restaurant owners managed and trained employees the same way no matter what type of restaurant they ran. When an employer decided it was time to train a dishwasher or anyone desiring to wait tables, age was not a factor because all went through an accurate step-by-step training. The method of step-by-step teaching taught waiters and waitresses to be efficient and how to think and plan ahead for several tables of customers at one time.

A waitress in training followed an assigned experienced waitress step by step for one week. She followed her to each table of customers and observed everything she did from writing tickets correctly, calling the order into the kitchen, side work and learned how to carry and balance plates. The second week of training, the new waitress began waiting tables; with the experienced waitress following her step-by-step, correcting any mistakes the new waitress made. By the third week the new waitress was ready to wait tables on her own. This method of repetitious teaching set firmly in the employee's memory, guidelines that develop the skill of waiting tables. If the employee was unable to grasp what they had been taught by the end of two weeks this method of teaching screened out ones who did not have the aptitude for waiting tables.

Part of training was also learning how to operate a cash register and counting change back to a customer. Cash registers then did not subtract the total from the amount of money given by a customer and show how much change the customer receives. This was done manually and employers practiced daily with new employees until they learned.

In those days cash registers did not add tax either. Restaurants had tax sheets which showed how much tax to charge on an amount of money. The waitress was expected to add the customer's ticket, and then figure the tax on the total. Since calculators were not in use at this time, this was figured on paper or done mentally.

Anyone who handled money was taught when a customer pays, the amount they give lays on the ledge of the cash register until after the customer receives their change. It was done this way to prevent confusion and to protect the restaurant from being cheated out of money. Sometimes a customer is unsure of whether they gave a ten dollar bill or twenty dollar bill to pay for a ticket. With the money laying on the ledge it is easy to show to the customer.

An employee was also taught a cash register drawer is never left open and unattended, nor do you turn your back to an open drawer. If money falls to the floor an employee should leave their hand on the register while picking it up or shut the drawer and then pick it up. Paper money faces the same direction with the front side facing up. These items do not seem to be important in restaurants today but less mistakes are made with money when it is organized and time is not wasted straightening it out if this is done as it is taken.

Waiting tables is not limited to women only. The majority in the food service industry are women and minorities but men young or old can wait tables also. Most employers do not care whether they hire a male of female, as long as they can do the work correctly. Restaurant ads looking for employees will read, "need food service waiting staff or servers.' This does not limit it to women only. In this reference the word, server, will be used to indicate a waiter or waitress.

Public opinion is that anyone can wait tables but professionals know this is not true. It is a skill of grace and diplomacy. The basics can be learned in a few weeks but grace and diplomacy develops from years of experience.

The key to learning is repetition. A person first must know how to wait tables correctly. Whether it is a large or small restaurant specializing in a particular type of food, there are guidelines and rules to help any server become a professional.

Chapter Two
'Basic Guidelines and Rules'

* The first is, <u>the customer comes first,</u> but what does this mean? This means the customer is never ignored because servers are eating or busy doing something else. If you cannot attend to the customer immediately, tell the customer you will be with them momentarily.

* Treat all customers equally with good service whether they tip or not. Just because they do not tip the first time, doesn't mean they won't the second or third time. Tips are the main part of your income but genuine concern and caring is remembered long after the tip is gone.

* When you enter your workplace, wash your hands first and as often as possible throughout your shift.

* A server should make at least five to seven trips to a table. If working with a hostess or owner, he or she should bring menus and silverware first. If not, then bring these items to the table first.

    Step 1. Greet your customer and ask what they would like to drink. While you are preparing their drinks your customers will be looking over the menu. Most are ready to order by the time you return with the drinks.

    Step 2. Take their order and turn it into the kitchen.

Step 3. While their food is being cooked, prepare their table with butter, steak sauce, crackers, etc. and also refills on drinks. Don't make your customers ask for these things. This is immediately annoying. Reason, what would I like with my meal?

Step 4. Food goes out to the table along with refills on drinks.

Step 5. Check on your customers shortly after they start eating. Ask if their food is okay.

Step 6. When your customers are through eating, take their plates from the table. Refill their drinks and ask if they would care for dessert or anything else. Leave their guest check at this departure. Most customers at this point are either ready to leave or stay and visit with a companion. If they stay, check on them occasionally but do not be pesky. An overly anxious server can be just as annoying as a neglectful one.

* As soon as your food order is placed in the window take it out immediately to the customer. This should take precedent over anything else you are doing. Most cooks ring a bell to let you know the order is ready and will continue to ring it until you take the order out. They do not want the food to get cold, hard or crusty.

* Before you take your plates out, eye your plates briefly and make sure they are prepared correctly before taking them to a customer.

* Hold glasses at the bottom. Never touch the rim of a glass.

* The correct way to refill a glass or cup is to remove it from the table, fill it and place it back on the table. In this manner you do not lean in front of a customer or have a pitcher or coffee pot in their way. Drips go to the floor and not on the table or customer.

* Be mindful of refilling drinks. A first cup of coffee in the morning is normally drank quickly. It is the same with tea or water on a

hot day. If one table needs refills it is likely all your tables will. If possible try to refill all of your tables at the same time.

* When customers do not eat all of their food ask if anything is wrong, especially if it is meat. If nothing is wrong ask if they would like a to go box. Some people are embarrassed to ask for this.

* If a customer complains about the food it is best to take the plate back to the kitchen first and inform the cook or manager. In most cases when there is something legitimately wrong the customer is offered another dish to eat or is not charged, but it is the manager who decides this and not the server.

* Never argue with the cook if your plates are prepared incorrectly, but do not take them to the customers either. Politely explain to the cook what is wrong. Do not serve food you would not eat, like wilted salad or hard rolls.

* Never give your opinion on how a person likes to eat their food. Some like gravy on pancakes or saltines with oatmeal. We all have individual tastes and no one appreciates criticism.

* Do not carry items such as straws, silverware, bottles and etc. in your pockets.

* Do not waste. Items like wrapped crackers, straws, toothpicks and napkins cost. Steak sauce bottles should be drained one on top of the other. Gallon ketchup cans and gallon salad dressing jars should be scraped thoroughly. Keep in mind, a nickel's worth of this and that in the trash can break a restaurant.

* Unused wrapped items should be returned to the waitress or waiter station. These should not go to the trash can unless soiled. Napkins are used for eating only. Paper and cloth towels are used for wiping up messes.

* Keep your work area clean. Rinse coffee pots and wipe down counters. Pick up dropped food on the floor.

* Bowls should be carried with a liner under them. This is a salad plate or saucer. Bowls are hard to carry without one and you have to touch the rim of the bowl to place it on the table.

* When carrying plates of food or clean dishes, extend them from your body as much as possible.

* Use a tray to carry several plates of food or several glasses. Do not make endless and needless trips to a table.

* Your towel should be clean and rinsed every time you wash a table. Slide or remove sugar, salt and pepper bottles aside and wash under these. Wipe the outside of sugar, salt and pepper bottles and place them in their correct position. Wash along the sides of the table and the seat of a chair or booth. Children in particular leave greasy or sticky handprints. Do not wipe crumbs to the floor. If food has been dropped to the floor, pick it up and place the chairs back to their correct positions at the table.

* For years customers were always served ice water no matter what they drank, but because of cost many restaurants have stopped serving water unless requested. Water, however, still needs to be served with certain beverages. Always with coffee, hot tea, juice and milk.

* When customers order milk most prefer that it stay refrigerated until their meal is ready.

* Do not pack a glass full with ice for a beverage unless the customer requests this.

* Never walk anywhere empty-handed. There are always clean dishes to bring up or dirty ones to take back. There are always items that need to be stocked. 'Make your steps count!'

* Try to make the next person's job easier. For instance, scrape dishes for the dishwasher. Write hard and clearly on a guest check. This makes it easier for the cook to read. If you see something that needs to be done, do it.

In today's styles of casual clothing it is easy for a server to look sloppy especially for the younger generation when a uniform is not specified. Prior to the mid 1960's all restaurant employees wore white uniforms and white shoes. Female cooks wore hairnets and waitresses wore their hair up or back, heavily sprayed with aquanet hairspray. A year to two years later waitresses were allowed to wear black dress uniforms with black shoes.

Through the years styles have certainly changed. Restaurant employees wear an array of colors and caps. Clothing and shoes are cute and trendy. Caps have replaced hairnets and hairspray. Many waitresses wear their hair loose and down.

The newer styles are good and bad. Mostly it seems this has caused a lot of confusion as to what is appropriate attire for restaurant employees. Appearance is the first thing your customer sees. This immediately gives a good or bad impression. Since clothing is no longer a rigid issue in restaurants, there are still a few basic guidelines the public expects to see in your appearance.

Baggy or hip hugging jeans are not appropriate nor t-shirts with the exception of a t-shirt with the business logo. Clothes and shoes should look neat and clean and preferably pressed. The standard black slacks and white shirt or blouse looks elegant and classy even in a small restaurant. Long hair should be up or back and lightly sprayed to prevent it from falling out. Jewelry, make-up and nail polish should be modest. More and more shorts are acceptable but short-shorts are not. Remember you are going to work and not to the beach. Although they are not flattering, most employers require shorts to be knee length. Sleeveless clothing and open-toed shoes are unsafe to work in because of hot grease and food. Visible armpits seem unsanitary and ask yourself, "Do you want to see someone's armpits and toes when you are eating?"

Good posture is a part of restaurant training as well as appearance. Always stand up straight because this will help your back from the pounding restaurant walking does to it. Never lean over in front of a customer and always kneel down to pick something up.

* Don't be a phony. Some servers think being overly friendly will get them more tips. Excessive talking, flirting or provocative

clothing may get you more tips but this gives a poor impression of you and the business you work at.

* Do not squat at a table, put your leg up on the seat or sit with a customer while taking their food order. This is very unprofessional. Be yourself and give good service and you will earn well.

* Always smile and say hello. Keep in mind while customers are waiting for their food they are watching you work. So be cheerful.

* Personal problems stay at home. Your mood shows and will provide a positive or negative influence to everyone around you.

* Never gossip about co-workers, customers, or employers. This kind of person is a trouble maker and good employers will not tolerate this type of employee.

* Do not chew gum while you are working.

* It is a natural response to brush hair out of your face when it falls and to moisten your fingertips with your tongue when handling guest check tickets but try to consciously avoid doing this.

* When walking up to a group of people praying at their table stop and wait until their prayer is finished before proceeding to serve them. This shows respect.

* Dirty ashtrays should be wiped out with a used napkin and placed back on the table. Periodically they should be washed. If they are being constantly washed then you will be continuously running to find ashtrays for customers.

* All restaurant employees should not park their vehicles in spaces designated for customers.

* Be courteous to everyone around you whether it is customers, co-workers or salesmen.

There was a time in restaurants if a food ticket was not written correctly the cook would not prepare the order until the ticket was corrected. It was the same with verbal orders. The words, "I need", were never used in turning orders into the kitchen.

Speed is very important in writing tickets for the front and kitchen. All words are abbreviated because it takes a lot of time to write out every item a customer orders. It also takes a lot of time for a cook to read. Meat is written first on a ticket because it takes longer to cook. Potatoes, vegetables, bread and other side dishes are prepared in advance and it is not necessary to write all of this. Drinks and desserts are written at the bottom of a guest check so that this does not confuse a cook. If a customer wants changes on the plate a simple - or + sign is very effective. Some use the symbol / which means, cut, to indicate a change. For example: -pot (potato) + sal (salad), /tom (cut tomato) or ø (cut onion). Meats are easier to abbreviate than vegetables. Example: CF (Chicken Fried Steak), H.B. (Hamburger). Some restaurants number meals on menus. On those all you would write is the number of the meal such as a #6, #3, etc. Chain restaurants try to develop more efficient ways for ordering food using computers or printing guest checks with menus. On those you write a check sign or cross in a small box beside an item. Writing tickets is still the most widely used today and is part of learning to wait tables correctly.

Servers need to be fast to wait on several tables at one time but if this is not done correctly speed is a waste. Concentrate repetitiously on these guidelines daily as you work first, and speed will come with time.

T.I.P.S. means To Insure Proper Service.

Chapter Three
"Sidework"

Sidework is basically preparation. Every day tea, coffee and a variety of beverages are prepared by servers in restaurants all over the country for busy breakfast, lunch and dinner runs. Lemons are sliced and desserts are cut to serve quickly and efficiently. Before a busy run begins and after it is over, all condiments, bottles and silverware should be cleaned, filled and rolled. Ice is brought up, and water and tea pitchers are full and ready to use. If you discover you are out of a particular type of salad dressing or anything else notify your employer before the run begins. Depending on the type of restaurant you work in, it will be your responsibility to prepare certain food items. Do not wait until the last minute to do these preparations. For a profitable and smooth run these items must be done in advance.

Servers should be on the floor and ready to start taking orders from customers ten minutes before shift change. This allows the server preceding you to complete their side work in preparation for the following shift. This includes the shift that closes at night. The restaurant should be left clean and all condiments and bottles filled, and silverware rolled for the next morning.

Throughout your shift along with general cleaning, your employer will require you to help with deeper cleaning. Busy restaurants become dirty very quickly. Windows, doors, refrigerators, walls, and tables and chairs need to be cleaned periodically. Salt and pepper shakers, sugar bowls and any bottle that holds sauces are touched by many hands daily. These items need to be washed on the outside every day.

Restaurant work is physically tiring. Employers do expect employees to sit down and rest at times or take a break. Some employers assign break times but others do not. Most employees try to take a break before a run begins. Normally this is when you will eat. However, a run sometimes starts earlier than expected. Your partner server will cover the floor while you eat but be conscious of your co-worker's and customers needs. Remember, the customer comes first. Do not ignore business or your work because you are eating.

Restaurant towels are not called rags nor is grease put in a fryolator, rather it is oil. Towels for the front should be kept clean and white. Thick terry cloth towels are normally used in the kitchen because they are more absorbent. Cotton linen towels are for use in the front. If one should become stained from ketchup or salad dressing this can be soaked out with bleach water. Most owners allow servers, cooks and dishwashers to use two to four towels per shift a day. Most restaurants use a laundry service and exceeding the towels the service provides cost more or you run out of towels before the service is due to return. Restaurant towels are folded into thirds and stacked. In this manner one can be taken quickly without causing the stack to fall.

Chapter Four
"The New Waiter or Waitress"

Whether you are an introverted or extroverted personality, waiting tables is a frightening experience the first time. That fear does go away but it is not unusual to feel overwhelmed from time to time by a stampede of hungry people the first year of waiting tables. Eventually that fear becomes an adrenaline high and you look forward to being very busy.

Restaurants are divided into sections for servers to work. Tables are numbered. If they are not literally then they are mentally. A server works his or her section of tables only. If it is not organized this way then there is confusion and customers missed being waited on.

Memory is your most important asset. Half of your serving work is memory. Originally in restaurants there was one guest check only and this was used for the customer's benefit. In those days a cook was never given a carbon guest check or kitchen check to remember a customer's order. The server called the order in through a window that divided the kitchen from the front. This is where food orders are placed for servers to pick up and take to customers then and today.

The server and cook remembered exactly what customers ordered. If this meant no onions on a hamburger or cottage cheese with a steak instead of a potato, everyone was trained to remember. Servers remembered what kind of salad dressing a customer wanted or that another did not want lemon with their tea. These items were never written. It was not uncommon for a good cook and server to remember twenty-five to fifty food orders at one time! The carbon guest check has made this easier but it has not decreased the use of memory that much.

A new server should not be given more than a few tables to work until he or she feels they are ready for more. Partly this is because the new server is nervous and trying to remember everything they have been told and taught. An experienced server knows how to back up their co-server's work but a new server does not. A new server needs to concentrate on turning orders in correctly, taking plates to customers and remembering to refill drinks.

Lack of eye contact with customers when taking their order shows disinterest to the individual. It is also bad manners. You will wait on a wide variety of customers. There will be some who will eat in your work place daily and those who eat there two to four times a week. Vacationers try to patronize good restaurants they find year after year. However brief your contact might be with a customer, when that person leaves he or she should feel you cared. They will make the effort to come back even if it is a year later. This will end up profitable for you and your place of business.

A server is a mediator between the cook, the public and the owner. If there is a problem with the customer, whether it is a mistake with food or something else, the server is normally the first to know. He or she is the one who approaches the cook or owner with the problem. It will also be the server most of the time that explains to the customer in an attempt to satisfy or pacify. And this is where the skill of grace and diplomacy begins to develop.

Never use the phrase, "that jerk stiffed me." This means the customer did not tip or the server may feel the tip was meager. Waiting tables is one-on-one contact with people. If you are there only for the money and do not enjoy the interaction with people then it would be best to go into a different line of work.

Customers have the right to request a particular server. This does not offend co-workers. However, attempting to take customers away from each other creates hostility, resentment and confusion.

Servers are also expected to run cash registers at times, particularly in smaller restaurants. Looking at a cash register the first time, appears difficult to operate but it usually takes a week or less to learn how to run one. New servers should not be expected to operate a register until after they have learned to wait tables correctly.

Chapter Five
"The Difficult Customer"

It used to be taught in every business, 'the customer is always right', but realistically this is not always true. Most customers are genuinely nice and reasonable people. They are more than willing to overlook mistakes, and mistakes are made from time to time even with the most experienced server, cook and owner.

It is best first to empathize with a customer's complaint. Treat the customer with importance. If you are making eye contact, the customer will see you are a caring person and will have the confidence in you to take care of his complaint.

You, as the server, do have the right to refuse service, just as your employer does to difficult and unruly people but this is said with caution. Most businesses do not want to lose customers and neither should you.

The negative thinking customer expects things to go wrong but when previous guidelines are followed this type is satisfied. There is also a type who gives all servers in every restaurant a difficult time. This type is usually subtle in their behavior and is trying to get the meal reduced in price or free. Sometimes an entire group or family is this way or it can be an individual. They will complain something is wrong with an item of food and/or keep you running to get extra things they want. One employer decided years ago the best way to handle this type was to charge extra. You can do this subtly by charging for bread, crackers, lemons, etc. These items are calculated into the price of a meal beforehand but customers do not know this. Or some employers will tack an extra $.50 to a $1.00 on each plate at the register when this type pays. An experienced server can spot this type quickly but it is easy for this kind to take advantage of a new server. If needed, a more experienced server or employer can take over their service.

Sexual comments from customers are best ignored. Responding to those comments in a casual or joking manner causes the individual to feel you are interested sexually. However, if a customer is too aggressive ask a more experienced server to take over their service.

Don't touch customers even if it is a friendship pat. They can get the wrong understanding. Or you can cause someone's wife or husband to feel jealous and angry. It is the same when joking with customers. Be careful what you say. Some people feel easily demeaned.

Another difficult customer you may wait on are derelicts. These are poor souls who have created a fantasy world to live in. They are usually hitchhikers no one wants around. They normally patronize interstate restaurants. They usually have no money or very little. They are hungry, tired and sometimes cold. Mostly they are looking for kindness. Some employers will feed them and send them on their way. Others offer them a little work for the price of a meal. The police will normally take them to a homeless shelter or some church organizations have temporary shelters.

Without these types of customers in your work day, there are still days when everything goes wrong. It is not uncommon for servers to spill drinks at a customer's table or for food to slide off a plate. These mistakes happen because an employee is in too big a hurry or may be feeling nervous. When this happens and you are feeling embarrassed, take a moment to regain your composure. Then try again.

Chapter Six
"Restaurants"

The word, restaurant, comes from the Latin word 'restaurure' meaning to restore. The first restaurants operated along roadsides where travelers stopped to rest and restore their energy. There are two main kinds of restaurants, full service and fast food.

Ethnic restaurants serve food of a specific country such as Mexico, China, etc. Gourmet restaurants offer menus that change daily and feature somewhat unusual menu choices. Some also feature classical dishes prepared from recipes created by great chefs. These meals are costly.

Fast food restaurants are not full service restaurants nor is food prepared in the same manner. Many of these restaurants offer salads or a salad bar for nutritional value. Fast food restaurants have their own training program and basic serving skills are not used in these restaurants.

Cafeterias prepare nutritional meals but these are self-service as fast food restaurants are. Many full service restaurants offer an all-you-can-eat buffet along with a salad bar as well as a full menu to order from. Although a customer does prepare their own plate a customer is given full service.

The largest number of restaurants are family restaurants which sell food at a moderate price. As more and more wives work today, eating out is a booming business. It has been said, 'there will always be restaurants and bars', and this is truer today than in the past. It is even common today to see convenience stores sell freshly cooked food or baked pastries and to provide seating.

People who eat out daily prefer a family restaurant. Up to the 1970's many of these restaurants were called café's or diner's. The word, café, means coffee, and the word, diner, is someone who dines. Diners used to resemble a dining car. To modernize restaurants, through the years the words, café and diner, became almost obsolete. Today some restaurant owners name their restaurant café or diner to denote a nostalgic and home-like environment.

These restaurants can be fairly large or small and basically serve a variety of food. These restaurants can be a mixture of ethnic and American food or American food only. Some specialize and some do not. In family restaurants the food is simple, fresh and home cooked. The environment is comfortable and people are generally friendlier.

Restaurant work, food, customers and owners have changed through the years. It used to be a treat to get to go out and eat. Now it is commonplace. Working men used to traditionally eat meat, potatoes and beans. This has been replaced with chicken breasts and salads. People today are health conscious because of obesity and cholesterol. They still eat their favorite foods but they try to, at least part of the time, eat healthy. Breakfast used to be the most important meal of the day. Now, it is a biscuit from a drive-thru restaurant, donut or maybe a bowl of cereal. People today look forward to eating breakfast at their favorite restaurant on the weekends.

Whatever kind of restaurant you work in; learn all you can about the food you serve. Customers always ask what is in a dish, how it is cooked or what comes with it. If you don't know, go ask. Never lie to a customer. Do not recommend food you do not feel is good. If food is under cooked, over cooked or not seasoned correctly tell the cook or owner so this can be corrected. However, when customers ask questions about the food, they are not asking for your personal taste. Restaurants sell food and service and whether you like the food or not, is not important as long as it is prepared correctly.

It is primarily chain restaurants that train their employees. Many restaurants do not offer training and are reluctant to hire inexperienced employees. Those that are hired, are not trained correctly because many of the newer employers do not have the years of experience to train. In the past, owners trained or assigned training step-by-step.

Chapter Seven
"A Server's Equipment"

A restaurant is designed for fast efficient service in the kitchen as well as in the front. Equipment is placed in a particular spot for speed. For the server, they have an area called the waiter or waitress station. In this station menus, silverware, glasses, cups, water, a coffee machine and a buscart are kept. Also a small tub for clean hot water, plus a cola machine and a tea container. Where possible a small refrigerator is placed here or near the station for holding ketchup, butter, lemons, dressings, etc. These areas differ in space from restaurant to restaurant but this is the area which most of your work is done from.

A buscart is a server's right arm. They are used by every employee in a restaurant and are made to save time, steps and work. A buscart is designed with three shelves for holding dirty dishes, a trash bin on one end and a small tub on the other for hot soapy water and a towel. Buscarts are used to clean tables quickly. Glasses, cups and silverware are placed in a tub on the top shelf. Dirty plates and trash are scraped into the trash bin and put on the second and third shelves. The towel is easily reached for washing the table and can be rinsed quickly if it is necessary to wash the table a second time.

Every restaurant needs two because more than one person will be cleaning tables. Buscarts can be used to carry several plates of food to large groups of customers. Buscarts are used in kitchens to carry heavy cases of food and are wheeled into large walk-ins for removing large items of foods. Buscarts provide space for dishwashers when there is not an area to place dirty dishes and can be used to carry clean dishes.

When a server does not use a buscart to clean tables with, they make numerous trips to the dishwashing area carrying dishes they may possibly drop and break. The server loses time, speed and causes their work to be harder.

A few years ago a waitress broke her arm but with the aid of a buscart was able to continue waiting tables with little time off work. With her good arm she lifted plates of food onto a buscart and pushed orders to customers. Because buscarts are used frequently they should be kept clean and presentable to the public.

A restaurant apron for a server is made to look attractive and serviceable. Younger waitresses more than waiters feel an apron takes away from the appearance of their clothing and do not want to wear one. If their employer insists they wear one then the server will choose an apron that is too tight and impractical for waiting tables. A guest check book and pen should be on the server at all times when they are waiting tables. For servers that do not wear aprons their guest check book and pen lays on a counter somewhere in the restaurant and before the server can take an order they have to stop and go find it.

When a server carries a guest check book and pen in their pants pockets or a tight apron they have difficulty pulling these items quickly from these types of pockets. Real restaurant serving aprons are made with large loose pockets. They are made this way for speed and efficiency. The apron ties should not be wrapped around the waist and tied in the front. Servers write just as much as they walk and it should be easy to pull a guest check book from pockets.

In past years most restaurants provided uniforms, aprons or smocks with pockets but through the years stopped this because of the expense. Today, employers do have a policy of what employees wear but the cost goes to the employee. Often the employee has the choice of design and when the employee has little or no experience they do not know clothing can hinder their efficiency as a server because they will choose style over practicality.

Restaurant dishes are heavier than the dishes used for home use. Restaurant dishes distribute heat evenly for food and they are also made for balance. Older servers know how to carry six to eight plates balanced, to a table without dripping or spilling. It is the same with glasses and cups. It takes a few weeks of practice to learn how to position dishes in certain areas of your hand, fingers and wrist. In restaurants today younger servers are not taught this. Instead they are taught to carry dishes on a tray and this is more practical than carrying three plates at a time to a group of eight customers. If you do not know how to balance dishes use a tray. This speeds service to customers but trays have to be positioned and balanced correctly because if they are not it is easy for a glass to tip over or for food to spill.

Chapter Eight
"Your Co-Workers"

A hostess makes a server's work easier. A hostess can be a male or female. Their job basically is to run the cash register. In some restaurants the hostess balances and totals the register before and after a shift. Some employers like to have one person responsible for money because when there are two or three people running a register mistakes are made with money. When there is only one then less mistakes are made.

A hostess seats customers, brings menus and sometimes silverware. He or she might also inquire as to what the customer would like to drink. If it is busy in the restaurant and the hostess has time he or she will prepare drinks for the server to take to customers. A hostess does not take orders from customers. If this does happen then the server needs to be informed immediately to prevent confusion. A hostess is not hired to wait on tables. They are paid minimum wage or more and are not entitled to tips.

When restaurant employers start trying to cut back on costs, the hostess position is the first to go. Employers take the place of the hostess for breakfast, lunch and dinner runs. In slower times servers or a trusted server runs the cash register. A good employer does not expect servers to operate a cash register during busy runs because service to customers is the priority of a server. This is what they are taught and trained to do. Most servers would rather not touch the cash register because this breaks their concentration and organization in service to customers especially when they have several tables to wait on.

Old timer restaurant owners would yell at a server if they saw a used napkin in a cup or glass. So would the dishwasher. Although it is a very common practice today it is a bad habit in restaurant work. It is a basic rule to try to make the next person's job easier and this includes the dishwasher. It is not acceptable to pile plates, glasses, cups, silverware and trash into one tub on a buscart or for this to be carried back to a dishwasher this way. If this is done because a server is to busy to scrape and organize dirty dishes on a buscart, then this should be done as soon as the server has a free minute. This increases speed for the dishwasher and is cleaner. A good dishwasher will help bus tables or help in the kitchen during a run but he or she cannot do this if they are too busy sorting out a mess.

In larger busier restaurants a busboy or girl is hired to clean tables. Because their job is considered meager it is customary for servers to give them a portion of tips in appreciation for the help they give.

In restaurants that open at 6:00 a.m., a dishwasher's shift may not begin until 9:00 a.m. or later. It is the same on an evening shift. Employers schedule like this to cut down on salaries. The cook, server and sometimes the employer washes dishes until the dishwasher arrives. A restaurant front should not be left unattended but if there is another server there or an employer is in the front, a server can run a load of dishes through an automatic dishwasher without being gone from the front but a minute or two.

The dishwashing area should be kept clean. A garbage disposal is not made for anything and everything to be ground up. A disposal will stop up or a plumbing line. A restaurant garbage disposal is made with a high pressure sprayer over it. This is used to spray excess food off dishes after food is scraped into the trash. Dishes then are placed into a commercial dishwashing tray and ran through the dishwasher. Many owners put screen traps over disposals to prevent large amounts of food and plastic from being ground up.

Some buscart tubs are made with a silverware compartment. This is filled with hot soapy water and is used for soaking dirty silverware. If this kind of tub is not available then a gallon can is used for this. Soaking silverware prior to washing helps to get it cleaner and prevents silverware from looking spotty. Automatic dishwashers do not remove lipstick off the rims of glasses and cups nor dried egg on plates. These have to be wiped with a wet towel before washing. It is easy to miss seeing silverware fall into a trash can when servers or dishwashers are hurriedly scraping plates. This costs the employer money and some will go through the trash looking for lost silverware. They will also caution employees to be careful not to lose silverware.

It is a rule in restaurants that if you make a mess you clean it up yourself. Dishwashers are good to clean up messes but if servers expect this every time then a dishwasher will feel a server is lazy and won't help. It is the same when using refrigerated items such as ice cream. Put these items back immediately and do not expect others to do this for you.

Waiting tables is stressful during a busy run but this stress is greater on a cook who is trying to prepare fifty orders at one time. In an evening run, customers are not in a hurry and are prepared to wait half an hour for their food order. However, a lunch run is the opposite. People have thirty minutes to an hour for a lunch break. This is why restaurants feature lunch specials that are prepared in advance or a buffet line for a lesser price than what is on the regular menu. Still, there are days customers do not want specials or a buffet. Instead they will want something different. When this happens a server needs to inform the customer whatever particular food they ordered takes longer to prepare just in case the customer does not have time to wait. This is wise to do anytime you know an order takes longer to cook than normal. If a customer is prepared to wait then he or she does not become irritable waiting and wondering why their order is taking so long.

Restaurant cooking is very different than cooking at home. Although some people have a natural talent for cooking or baking or both, it takes years to master the skill of restaurant cooking. This skill is not fully developed from working in one restaurant only but comes from learning to cook in a variety of restaurants featuring different types of foods. Inexperienced cooks tend to hurry food preparation by flipping or turning cooking food repeatedly or by turning up the temperature. Experienced cooks prepare food with patience and allow food to cook naturally.

Most people learning to cook, start out as a back up cook. Basically the back up cook assists the head cook while they are being taught and trained. Until they gain experience, a back up cook's salary is lower than the head cook. Some older servers become cooks after years of waiting tables because they become, burned out, and no longer feel they can cope with the public.

Cooks have more side work or prep work than servers do. The prep work for ethnic cooking is double compared to the preparation for American food. On busy days it is difficult for a cook to do prep work and prepare orders for customers at the same time.

Good cooks try to prepare well balanced and nutritious meals. When deciding specials a good cook would never plan an all starch plate such as pasta, corn and potatoes with a meat. A green vegetable would replace at least one of the starches.

Cooks know how to time their plates so that all orders on a ticket are finished cooking at the same time. For example, if a cook had a well done steak and a rare steak on a ticket, the cook would begin cooking the well done steak before the rare one.

In every culture, people eat and prepare food differently which provides a variety of restaurants. In every restaurant there is something new to learn about food and preparation.

Cooks are considered more valuable to restaurant owners than servers. It is easier to replace a server than a cook. Servers never argue with cooks or order a cook around. If there is a dispute between a cook and a server, the cook has the final say. Cooks are entitled to a position of respect and a good owner will side with a good cook before a server.

Cooks primarily prepare the ordering list for food companies and some do the ordering. When servers see an item running low or out, they should inform the cook or write it on a list. This prevents items from being missed when ordering and time is not wasted trying to prepare a grocery list at the last minute.

No restaurant is dependent on one person. Every restaurant needs cooks, servers, dishwashers, busboys and hostesses, and each serves a purpose. Employees are organized this way to provide a product and service.

A competitive person works independently. Working with this kind of individual makes everyone's job difficult and unpleasant. This kind of employee does not realize they cannot do their job alone. Every employee is dependent on each other.

It is important that each employee work the job they were trained and hired to do. When cooks try to do a server's job or a dishwasher tries to do a hostess' work then confusion develops. There is nothing wrong in helping each other but don't forget what your assigned work is. A successful restaurant is well organized and employees are a part of the formula that makes it work.

Chapter Nine
"Restaurant Employers"

Sitting down and eating in a restaurant looks easy but the public has no idea of the organization it took to accomplish that feat. In the past twenty years one person after another opens a restaurant with no experience or very little in this field and often their business folds within six months to a year.

People are not born natural restaurant owners. Anyone considering buying a restaurant or managing one should work in one for a few years first. Owners need to know how to cook, wait tables, wash dishes and run a cash register because employees do call in sick or have emergencies come up and owners may have to fill one of these positions. An experienced owner knows there are hidden taxes in the restaurant business and food costs are continuously rising. An owner knows no two cooks prepare food alike and oversees the preparation of food. Owners also must know the area and public they are serving.

No one can work sixteen hours a day, seven days a week but this type of business is very demanding and confining. Even in an owner's 'off' time an owner is doing book work or running errands for the restaurant.

Successful restaurant owners do not schedule themselves to work a daily shift cooking or waiting tables. However, a new owner will cook for the first few weeks in a new business. Primarily this is to train and oversee the preparation of food. Owners need to be free in order to oversee and aid during busy runs. If orders are coming out of the kitchen slow, then the owner assists in the kitchen to help speed up orders. If servers are overrun with customers then the owner helps set up customers. It is the same with dishes. Owners work wherever they are needed most but they are especially needed to run cash registers when there is no hostess.

Running a cash register is to an owner's advantage, especially when it is busy in a restaurant because that is when the most mistakes happen. It gives an owner the opportunity to check tickets and make sure customers are being charged correctly. The public expects and wants to see an owner and customers want to hear an owner say, "was everything alright?" This makes the public feel the owner values them as customers and appreciates their business. In some sixteen to twenty-four hour restaurants there is a manager and assistant manager. The assistant's responsibility is the same as the manager's to oversee employees and food preparation.

Do not confuse a fast food restaurant manager with a full service manager. There is a big difference in training, food preparation and organization.

There are few restaurants where everyone is a good employee. Poor employees can become good employees through good management but for owners who are not there when they are needed, employees develop an 'I don't care' attitude.

Management does not have to be rigid to force employees to work hard. Sometimes, a little psychological profiling and learning one's limitations can develop a productive employee.

Good managers work just as hard as they expect their employees to, if not harder. They will not overload an employee with more work than they can do at one time. Good employers try to prevent waste and will take whatever steps are necessary to stop it.

Some restaurant owners will set a ridiculously low price on a breakfast or lunch special. They realize money will not be made from these specials but are trying to draw in business. They hope out of two customers, one will have the special and the other a higher priced menu choice. This seldom works financially well for an owner but it does draw business in and servers profit from this.

Restaurant owners are in the business to sell food and drinks and it is not up to a server to decide to give a customer a free piece of cake or anything else without the owner's consent. Owners do occasionally give food or drinks to customers at no charge but servers must follow the charging policy the owner sets.

The more simple the menu is, the less food cost there is to an owner. More money is earned from individual plates than a buffet and salad bar. Buffets are financially dependent on the quantity of customers. However, good buffets draw customers in and increase business.

Good owners know their limitations. This is why some restaurants are open for two meals a day instead of three. This could be for breakfast and lunch or lunch and dinner, or lunch or dinner only. Before an owner decides this he or she takes into account the area in which the business is in and what the public expects. When a new owner buys an already thriving restaurant and makes changes in food quality they will lose business or fail completely. It is alright to improve, but to take away is a costly mistake.

The first year a restaurant is open it is rare for it to make any real profit. Although restaurants make big money quick, the first year is spent building up business. Yearly, there are quarterly taxes, unemployment and liability insurance, workman's compensation and some hidden taxes. Monthly, there is a lease or building and equipment payment, utilities, food cost and supplies, salaries and social security employers have to match for employees. There are fees for licenses and unexpected expenses. Restaurants are considered a small business but there is nothing small about the cost to own and run one.

Inexperienced people buy restaurants for different reasons. One reason given is, 'they have always enjoyed working with food' and another is, 'they have always wanted to run their own business.' Some inexperienced owners believe the food they serve will be better than any other restaurant and customers will drive from fifty miles away to eat in their restaurant. Experienced owners simply hope to get their share of business and do not believe they will outdo any other restaurants. Inexperienced owners attempt to run a restaurant from preconceived ideas and because they lack practical working knowledge employees suffer.

Many new owners who can't make financial ends meet decide to start working serving shifts to earn money from tips. For many years, it was unheard of to tip an owner or manager. The public resents this because it takes away income from servers. Owners earn their money from the plates of food they sell in their restaurant business and to receive tips also, is earning a double income. In some restaurants, owners pay themselves a salary or their mate. This way the owner has an income to live on until the restaurant begins earning a profit.

Owners do not have the time or concentration to wait tables and run a business at the same time. They should not wait tables unless they do not have any servers. A good owner may help a server during a busy run but the owner is not doing this for tips nor does he or she keep tips. The owner is trying to ensure a good business.

Chapter Ten
"Organization and Safety"

People like to try out new restaurants. However, if they do not have a good impression the first time, there is a good chance they will not come back. Organization and timing is vital to running a successful restaurant. If the kitchen is prepared for business but the front is not, then poor service is given to the customers. It is the same when the front is ready but the kitchen is not. The dishwashing area is just as important because the front and kitchen have to have clean dishes quickly. You hope to feed a hundred or more customers through a lunch or dinner run but whether you have a few or many, every area must be organized and every employee trained and ready. It only takes one dissatisfied customer to give a restaurant a bad name because word of mouth is the most powerful form of advertising there is.

Restaurant equipment is placed in a position where it is easily accessible to work with. This not only increases efficiency but saves restaurant walking which is hard on feet, legs and back. When menus feature food choices and the restaurant is out of an item then customers feel the restaurant is inconsistent. When specials and buffets are designated to be ready at a particular time and are not, this is due to poor timing. Calculating the time it takes to prepare foods makes the difference between success and failure with customers. All restaurants run out of food items unexpectedly from time to time but this should be replaced as soon as possible. Customers are willing to wait on specials and buffets that are not ready on time once in awhile, but if this happens habitually they will take their business elsewhere. Restaurants must keep consistent open and closing hours whether they have business or not. People depend on restaurants to be open as they advertise to be.

Customers should complain to a restaurant owner when service or food is not what it should be. Most customers do not want to cause any trouble or to be rude, but when a problem is not brought to the owner's attention, it is not corrected. What happens instead, is the customer does not come back and this hurts the business in the long run.

Restaurant work is not considered dangerous but if safety rules are not followed accidents can happen. Fryolators, meat slicers, grills and knives can maim a person permanently if not used correctly.

Restaurant kitchen knives are very sharp and are kept that way because of constant use. Servers do use these knives occasionally in their work. Most people are taught growing up when using a knife always cut away from your body. Before using a restaurant kitchen knife, let an experienced cook show you how these knives are held in your hands. Cooks have been trained to cut, slice and chop a variety of foods quickly without cutting their hands.

Steel mesh gloves should always be worn when operating a meat slicer.

Servers rarely clean a restaurant grill or change oil in fryolators but you will be observing how this is done. Grills are cleaned with oil, rolled grill towels, grill bricks and sometimes a grill screen. A generous amount of oil is poured onto a hot grill, then a grill brick is rubbed up and down on the grill until all food residue is loosened. This is then scraped with a wide blade knife into a drain made at the front or side of the grill. Grills are then wiped with a grill towel.

Depending on the size of the fryolator used, hot oil is drained or poured from these into a bucket and carried to an oil drum or vat. Then the fryolator is scrubbed clean with hot soapy water and steel mesh pads. Whenever a cook is working with hot oil it is easy to get burns. Most restaurant owners insist cooks wear gloves when cleaning these items. Although gloves do help to protect skin they do not prevent all burns.

The most common accident in a restaurant is falling on a wet floor. Employees know to be careful on a freshly mopped floor but are not always aware that floors can be damp from high humidity and if they are not walking carefully can slip and fall. It is just as easy to fall from small patches of water that are made from fallen ice cubes on floors. When ice is noticed on the floor it should be picked up. If it has already melted it should be wiped up.

Chapter Eleven
"Conclusion"

Periodically all restaurants are visited by a state health inspector. New restaurants are required by law to have a state health license along with a state tax number. There is a fee for both of these licenses. Health inspectors check for cleanliness, temperature control in refrigerators, walk-ins, freezers and steam tables. Their main concern is for food safety but they also check the water temperature in automatic commercial dishwashers and sanitization. Every year or two a new guideline is brought out for restaurants to follow and the inspector brings this to the restaurant owner's attention.

Cooks, dishwashers, hostesses and servers all earn different salaries in a full service restaurant. Prior to 1982 servers earned minimum wage, plus tips. The government, in that year, decided tips were income and should be taxed. Since servers earn more than minimum wage in tips most employers pay little or no salary to servers.

Waiters and waitresses do earn good incomes and for all other restaurant employees that stay with an employer they receive raises. Chain company restaurants, whether fast food or full service, offer benefits and financial security. However, individually owned restaurants rarely do.

People enter restaurant work because it does not require a formal education. For some it is a temporary job until a better one comes along. For others it is a way to earn a living while attending college because restaurant hours are flexible. Many are in this field however, because they enjoy working in the food service industry. Whatever the reason, restaurant work brings you in contact with people from all over the world. It teaches you about people and their cultures. You learn diplomacy, fairness and compassion and whether you are there permanently or temporarily, what you learn will educate you in all aspects of life for present or future endeavors.

About the Author

The author started working in restaurants at age eleven as many people did in those times. Through the author's career in the food service business the author saw a need for professionalism and pride that is often lacking in today's food service employees.

www.ingramcontent.com/pod-product-compliance
Lightning Source LLC
Chambersburg PA
CBHW021939170526
45157CB00005B/2348